HOW TO
FIGHT TOUGH

HOW TO
FIGHT TOUGH

By LIEUTENANT WILLIAM
HARRISON (JACK) DEMPSEY

United States Coast Guard

and Frank G. Menke

One hundred action photos teaching
United States Commando fighting

Specially posed by Lieutenant Dempsey and Coast Guard experts

Published by Hillman Periodicals, Inc.

"*THIS is the toughest war of all time. We need not leave it to historians of the future to answer the question whether we are tough enough to meet this unprecedented challenge. We can give that answer now. The answer is yes.*"

—PRESIDENT FRANKLIN D. ROOSEVELT

In his 1942 Labor Day address to the nation.

THIS book is respectfully dedicated to American young men everywhere—young men who are fighting in every branch of the country's armed service to preserve free institutions against the onslaught of the Axis nations. Today, in a world fighting a war to the death, "Fight Tough" must be the creed of every good soldier. It is in the hope of helping the individual American fighter in uniform attain that state of physical preparation that this book was written with the consent and the approval of the United States Coast Guard.

LIEUTENANT WILLIAM HARRISON (JACK) DEMPSEY

MY ORDERS—"MAKE 'EM TOUGH!"

WHEN I was appointed Lieutenant in the United States Coast Guard, the job of Director of Physical Fitness was turned over to me, and I was told to start from scratch at the new Coast Guard station at Manhattan Beach, New York.

"It is up to you to work out a program and to instruct the youthful Coast Guardsmen in how to take care of themselves under all circumstances," I was told.

It struck me that a Coast Guardsman perhaps has more varied duties than any one in the armed services of the nation. He must be prepared to fight on land or sea; he takes part in combat duty, must be ready for all emergencies, and, in his duties as guardian of the coasts, he is certain to be confronted by perilous situations.

Others teach the youngster aspiring to become a Coast Guardsman what to do with knife and gun. I concluded that what I would teach the boys was how to take care of themselves when they were caught unarmed by an enemy with arms, as well as how to take care of themselves when confronted by an unarmed, but far more physically powerful foeman.

So the first thing I did was to order adequate equipment—boxing gloves, light and heavy punching bags, mats for the rings as well as ropes and stakes for the boxing-wrestling rings, etc., and get everything constructed in a hurry, so that no time would be lost in teach-

ing the boys what I felt they should know in order to extricate themselves from any dangerous position.

Lieutenant Bernard Mooney, one of the greatest boxing and wrestling teachers in this country, who has been with Ohio State University
for 18 years or so, became my first assistant. Bernard J. Cosneck,
who graduated in Physical Education from the University of Illinois,
and who was tutored in jiu jitsu by the greatest Japanese teachers of
the art, was added to the staff. So was Andy Filosa, who has been a
teacher of boxing, wrestling and free style combat on land and sea
for many years. Mario Ghisello, who fought under the ring name
of Matty Mario, became another member, and within a short time
I had a staff of 32 assistants—and we went to work.

NEW squads of rookie Coast Guardsmen arrive at Manhattan Beach
every day or so, and almost immediately become members of our
class. I am allowed to have them, as a usual thing, for about one
hour every morning and one hour in the afternoon. This means
driving them hard to acquire in a limited time a rather sizeable
measure of knowledge.

Our daily classes range from about 10 to better than 600, depending entirely upon the number that have arrived. It is, as can be
observed, quite impossible to have the entire class doing the same
thing at the same time, because some members may have just arrived,
while others are nearing "graduation" from Manhattan Beach to
some other place assigned them by the Commander.

Therefore, these classes are split out into separate units, each under
a different instructor, and while some may be doing their first morning
of roadwork, others will be going through their farewell drills.

I have always considered roadwork one of the best and quickest
ways of developing the lungs and the muscles. Such development
is extremely vital to any one who must go in for physical perform-
ance. Therefore, the boys get roadwork each morning. The first
afternoon or two, the rookies usually get nothing more than calisthenics. After that, the tempo increases.

They are taught how to punch the bag—and are kept at it so many
minutes each day. The boys are paired up and learn about boxing,

or, if they know the art, they are sharpened up as much as is possible within a month's time. They are paired up for wrestling matches, taught the different holds, and go to work on each other.

I have noticed that, for the most part, the boys are not too keen about this physical training during the first week. Most of them arrive with soft and flabby muscles, and the drilling they have to undergo during the other hours of their training doesn't give them much relish for additional strain on their muscles in my department.

But after about a week of this, a change comes. The boys, by this time, have recovered from most of the muscular aches; they get the spirit of athletic training. They run the roads as though they really like it. They are always ready for boxing, wrestling and the other drills, and it is just about then that we proceed to teach them the rough tricks which they can call upon if their lives are menaced by an enemy.

These tricks embrace boxing, wrestling, jiu jitsu, and plenty of the "Pier Six" style of fighting—the knock-down, drag-em-out type of brawl where no holds are barred, where no foul rules prevail, and where butting, heeling, gouging and fouls of the most savage kind are among the chief items of attack.

"Do not kill the enemy in any instance where it can be avoided" is one of the Coast Guard rules. "Bring the enemy back alive, so that he can talk—and tell."

So the boys are taught how to subdue any enemy without killing him—unless the emergency calls for killing.

"Speed—speed—speed!" That is what we constantly drill into the boys as we explain each trick and direct him through the motions. "Speed—speed—speed!" The difference between success of these tricks and failure, the difference between the capture of an enemy or that Coast Guardsman's death often will depend upon speed.

OF COURSE, the boys are permitted to go through the drills slowly until they have learned every move they are to make. If they are slow to grasp the idea, we never are impatient with them. We know they'll acquire the knack after a time. Then they gradually increase the speed of the action, faster and faster. Usually, in the final drills, they do not work against each other. The instructor comes in. He poses as the enemy, and the youngsters try to disarm him.

Some of the boys are such apt pupils, and they are so fast in their movements, that even the best of our instructors have to call on the ultimate of their own speed, and all their cunning, to save themselves from coming off second best. We always make a memo of such boys, and pass it along. It is possible that if they are moved to other stations, for further drilling there in the arts of war, they may find appointment to handle small squads themselves.

It is not our thought that within a month's time we can school all rookies who come to us in more than the rudiments of boxing and wrestling, nor in the tricks that will enable them to subdue an enemy. We rush them along as hard and as fast as we can, hopeful that when they go to other stations, and take up their duties there, that in their leisure time they will pair off and continue to practice what they learned at Manhattan Beach. If they do that, then the boys in the U. S. Coast Guard can take rank with the roughest, toughest and most superb group of all-around fighting men on this earth.

They'll never need to take a backward step from anybody, any-where, under any conditions. And, if they always will remember the importance of speed of movement, more speed, and still more speed—if they will try to flash like lightning—each will be able to whip his own weight in wild cats, or anything else.

Now, to borrow the parlance of the prize ring, we have heard the ten second signal, and we are ready for the opening bell. We answer the gong, so to speak, with our hands up for protection, our eyes and ears wide open.

The trick in gouge fighting, just as in any other type of combat, is to expose the enemy's weakness first, to beat him to the punch, and to hit hard. These are reliable lines of procedure for my instruction in roughing up the Axis.

In the subsequent chapter, I explain the first of the many fighting tricks by which the Coast Guardsman is taught to render his enemy helpless.

—Lieutenant William Harrison Dempsey.

COMMANDO tutors of the United States Coast Guard. Left to right are Bernard J. Cosneck, Chief Bo'sn's Mate; Lieutenant Dempsey, boss of the outfit; Lieutenant Bernard F. Mooney, and Andy Filosa, Chief Bo'sn's Mate. The three men with the former world's heavyweight boxing champion are his chief assistants.

The total staff, including Dempsey, usually averages 33, but is occasionally smaller, as some of the best men are sent to other stations to impart the knowledge they have acquired under Lieutenant Dempsey at the Coast Guard's main headquarters in Manhattan Beach, New York.

All Dempsey's aides have impressive backgrounds which fit them well for their positions. Cosneck graduated from the University of Illinois in 1934 as a physical education teacher. Winner of the Big Ten wrestling championship in 1932 and 1934, he is one of the six men in the United States who learned the jiu jitsu methods as taught by the Six Degree Black Belt Japanese specialists.

Mooney taught wrestling and boxing at Ohio State University for 18 years. And Filosa, likewise a veteran professor of the art of self defense, has taught boxing, wrestling, jiu jitsu and general calisthenics in the U. S. armed forces for more than 15 years. He was in convoy work up until the time we entered the war.

OUT of his fighting togs into the uniform of the United States Coast Guard, Lieutenant Dempsey reports for duty at the Manhattan Beach training station. He receives his orders—and congratulations—from Captain G. U. Stewart, Commandant of the Manhattan Beach · Training Station, left, and Commander A. G. Hall, executive officer

★ ★ ★ ★ ★ *Contents* ★ ★ ★ ★ ★

(Note to the Reader: The emblems which appear at the head of each chapter are various Coast Guard insignia. They are published to enable the public to recognize the rank of Coast Guardsmen. They have no connection with the chapter pages on which they appear, nor do they illustrate or relate to the contents of this book in any other way.)

THIRD CLASS SEAMAN

THE COATSLEEVE HOLD

NOT all enemies are armed—but that doesn't mean they are not dangerous. In this war, where individual resourcefulness plays such a vital role, treachery on the part of the foe has been the rule rather than the exception. This is as true of individual Axis behavior as it is of Axis strategy.

There is no time for talk. Every second's delay increases your peril. You must take control of the situation with lightning rapidity. That means you must take control of the enemy, for the first advantage invariably turns out to be the most important.

The enemy, in this set of photos and others that follow, is one of my assistants, Bernard Cosneck, Chief Bo'sn's Mate, a specialist in improved jiu jitsu.

AS THE enemy comes forward, reach quickly for the lapels of his coat. Snap the shoulders, and back of the coat, forward and upward away from him. This gives you clearance for the next movement, which is very vital.

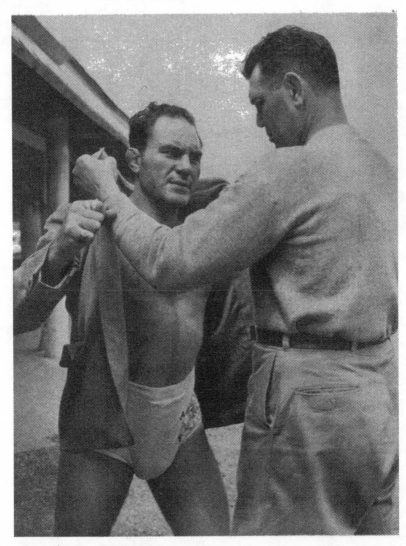

THE extent of the advantage you have thus gained becomes apparent as, moving with split-second speed, you jerk the coat backward and down under his arms. By taking such a quick initiative you have so far prevented him from acting against you.

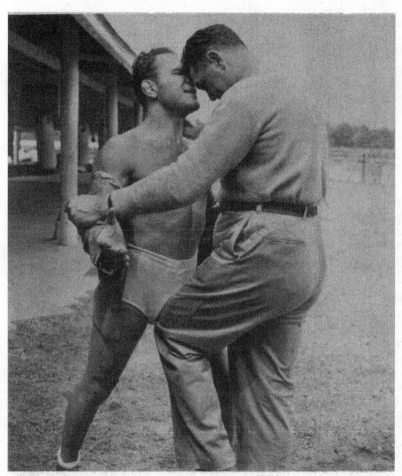

YOUR maneuver on the previous page locks your enemy's arms and renders them thoroughly helpless. Seizing upon this advantage, you manage in the same motion to drive your forehead into his face, and kick him in the groin with whichever knee happens to be closest to the groin. By now it should be apparent that wars are not fought according to the Marquis of Queensberry rules, so if you had any such dangerous notion now is the time to get it out of your mind. Alley fighting is strictly in order.

YOU'VE got the enemy pretty well on the run, but you must be quick to follow up your lead. If he isn't sufficiently helpless, don't hesitate to kick him in one or both shins. Then shift your left leg back of his left leg, never relaxing your hold on his coatsleeves.

NOW you've got him over a barrel, so you trip him to the ground. And you don't bother to see if there are any rocks there before you drop him. In war you fight for keeps, and the niceties of peacetime become weaknesses which the enemy will not hesitate to exploit in order to kill you. Throughout this exercise, as long as you keep his arms locked in the coatsleeves, he is completely at your mercy. Again I want to emphasize that this trick, like all others, depends for success upon speed of movement. Never forget that for one second. Speed—speed—and more speed.

SECOND CLASS SEAMAN

COLLAR GRAB

I N THE preceding exercise, I showed one way of handling an un-armed man who is wearing a coat, or any jacket with lapels. I am going to demonstrate still another method in this exercise.

Coast Guardsmen practicing the trick illustrated in the first two pictures that follow do so in a moderate way, so as to get the knack of the move. They do not try to put on the pressure in practice, lest it prove harmful.

The third, fourth, fifth and sixth photos in this group demonstrate how to break the strangle—an extremely important maneuver if you fail to gain the initiative as indicated in the two illustrations which precede.

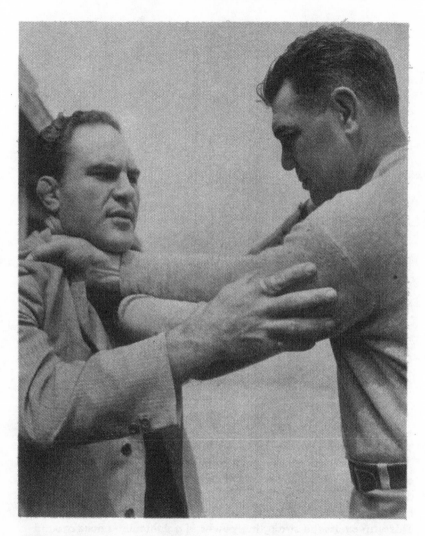

ASSUME that the enemy is arguing with you. He is about to make a grab for you, or take a punch at you. He won't get to first base if you cross your hands and beat him to it by making a fast lunge for both sides of his coat collar just under his ears. This is what is literally known as pinning the enemy's ears back.

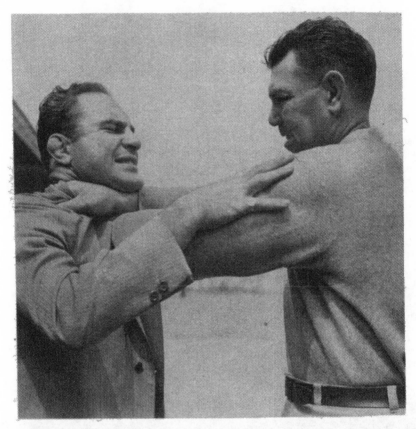

WHEN you take this hold, the inside of your wrists are facing each other. Then you simply twist your wrists toward each other, so that the insides are facing the ground. This puts tremendous pressure on the carotid arteries, preventing the blood from leaving or entering the head, and causing unconsciousness. This grip exerts the strangling power of a tightening noose around the opponent's neck. I caution all students not to overdo this in practice, because this is so effective a trick that it can easily prove harmful when you do not wish it to. Conversely, in actual combat with the enemy, you cannot possibly overdo it. Do it first. Do it right. And do it until your captive falls before your feet.

FOR the remainder of this exercise, I am going to dwell upon the art of breaking the strangle. A Coast Guard who employs the dangerous Commando tactics must naturally expect to take it as well as dish it out. The point is that even when you're forced into defensive action, it must be aggressive action. So aggressive, as a matter of fact, that defense becomes a misnomer in the flicker of an eyelash.

If the enemy puts a front stranglehold on you, it will make you uncomfortable only so long as it takes you to swing into hold-breaking action. After that, as I will show you, a few deft movements on your part will reverse the tables, and you will have him at your mercy. In this photo, he has both hands gripping your throat. While you are in that position, you cannot smash him in the groin with your knee, nor can you reach him with a kick in the shins. He is too far away.

YOU take your adversary by surprise and shoot both hands and arms—with all the brute force and lightning speed at your command—between his arms. If a few of his teeth happen to fall out in the process, don't bother feeling sorry for him. Remember: He'd kill you as soon as look at you!

C ONTINUING the upward motion **started in the previous pic-** ture, lift your arms and smash at **his arms with your own** in an outward movement. Don't pull **your punches. Administer this** rebuff with all the force of which you are capable. **It will break the** stoutest hold if delivered quickly enough.

D ON'T waste any time. Now bring your arms down fast with
the palms of your fist open, and the hands rigid. Slash down
at the sides of his neck and hack away. Hard and ruthlessly,
mind you. Show no mercy. Blows like this will jar him to his
heels. To aid your cause still further, kick him in the groin with
either knee. Kick him there with all the power you can summon.
Remember—your job is to put him out of commission.

FIRST CLASS SEAMAN

THE HEAD CLAMP

HERE is another trick being taught to the rookies in the U. S. Coast Guard for use when neither the enemy nor yourself has a weapon of any kind, and wherein you can win the impending clash—if you act with speed and accuracy of movement.

The thing to remember, the Coast Guard boys are told, is that whenever suspicion has been aroused, go into action at once. Render the enemy, or supposed enemy helpless, and explanations, if necessary, may be made later.

I AM in an argument with a supposed enemy, who, in this case, is my assistant, Bernard Cosneck. There is no time for make-believe. This is serious, grim business. If I don't act first, he's going to try to knock me out. So I make a fast grab for the back of his head with my left hand, and shove down on his head, so that I can clamp my right elbow, forearm and hand under his throat.

HERE is the telling result of this prompt and forceful action. My right forearm is under Cosneck's throat, choking him. My left hand is pressing at his shoulder blade. Were I to hold Cosneck in such a position for 15 to 30 seconds, exerting full pressure, he would collapse from strangulation. Commandos must get accustomed to seeing the breath peter out of their adversaries if they wish to go on breathing themselves.

PETTY OFFICER THIRD CLASS

SUBDUING AN ARMED ENEMY

WE'VE disposed, for the time being, of the unarmed enemy. If you had to be tough with him, you have to be a thousand times tougher—and quicker—with the armed foe. For no Jap or Nazi is going to scruple about pumping lead into your belly or smearing his bayonet with your blood. This is a branch of the service for men with guts from toe to head. Make no mistake about it. But the guts of a Coast Guardsman must be implemented with agility and resourcefulness. Courage alone is not enough to carry a Commando through. It may make him a hero—but a dead one. My training on how to get tough is geared to hit Uncle Sam's mortality list in the solar plexus. Our specialty is live heroes. That's why we insist, time and again—on brain work and speed. I drill my men on the importance of swiftness of motion until they perform every act instinctively, their reflexes springing into movement before their mind has time to consciously absorb the situation.

WATCH this closely. Your life may depend upon it some day.
The enemy points his gun at my chest. In the flash of a
second he can pull the trigger and blot me out of existence. What
can I do in that same flash of a second? Things look very black
indeed for me. But am I really helpless?

I AM raising my hands as he has ordered; BUT, notice that I am raising the right hand faster than the left. There is a very important reason for that. If I raised both at the same level, I would collide with my own hands, and spoil any chances for disarming the enemy.

IN RAISING the left hand, I raise it as close to the other man's gun hand as possible. When I am a few inches from it, and a few inches above (see previous photo), I make a downward grab with my left hand for the barrel of the gun. As you can see, I have grasped the top of the man's gun and twisted it away from pointing at me. After this, I can do one of several things.

I CAN hit him on the jaw, as I do in this picture, or I can give him the knee in the groin as I do in the next picture. If I continue twisting the gun, I will break his trigger finger because it is caught in the guard, and I will continue if need be.

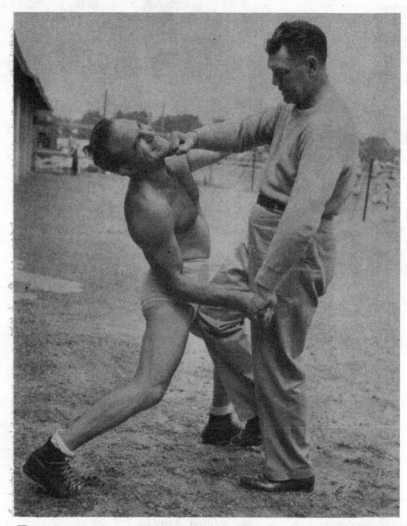

I F HE is close enough, I can punch him and give him the knee
at the same time. Or I can kick him in the shins. One form of
attack, or the other, will loosen the gun from his hands, and the
punching, kneeing or shin-kicking will take enough fight out of
him to enable me to subdue him with other holds.

PETTY OFFICER SECOND CLASS

A GUN IN YOUR BACK

DON'T expect always to see your enemy coming, armed or unarmed. The element of surprise is an important factor in Commando warfare. Just as you can use it to your immense advantage, so you can be victimized by it if it is employed by your enemy.

It is not uncommon for the enemy to sneak up on you from behind. That has been the history of Nazi and Jap warfare. So a Coast Guardsman must, of course, be prepared to cope with this type of threat.

In the previous exercise I demonstrated how to disarm a man who has a gun pointed at the chest. This exercise deals with disarming an enemy who has a gun pointed at my back. Look at the next page and pay very careful attention.

THE enemy, still posed by Bernard Cosneck, orders me to throw up my hands. But first I lean back so that the gun will touch my back. In that way I will know the exact place at which it is aimed. At the same time, it will make it harder for my captor to change the position of the weapon. What follows after that depends upon the rapidity of movement. Never, for one solitary second, lose sight of that: rapidity of movement! Always speed! If I am slow, I'm very liable to get a bullet in my back. But if I am fast to the absolute limit—and the boys at the Coast Guard are trained in speed and alertness—I am safe.

INSTEAD of raising my hands—or, if I want to be cagy, as I raise my hands—I whirl with lightning movement to my own right. My right elbow leads in the twirl, and is the first part of my body which touches his gun arm. This immediately puts my body out of the line of fire. My right arm continues in the original underhand motion, encircling the gun arm, and bending back at the elbow. This is the beginning of the end for him.

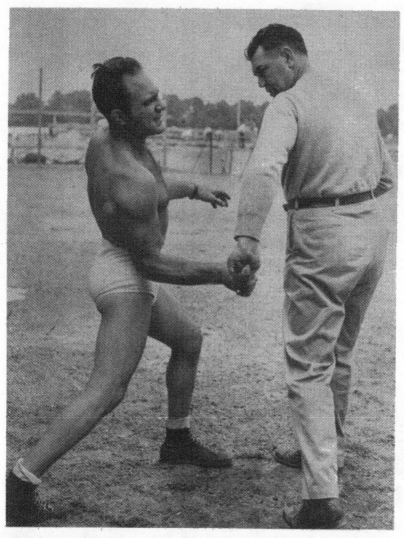

EVEN as I am pivoting, as the previous photo demonstrates, I have moved my right arm so that it is under that of the man with the gun. That enables me to lift the right arm, clamp it over the elbow of the enemy, and grab at the gun.

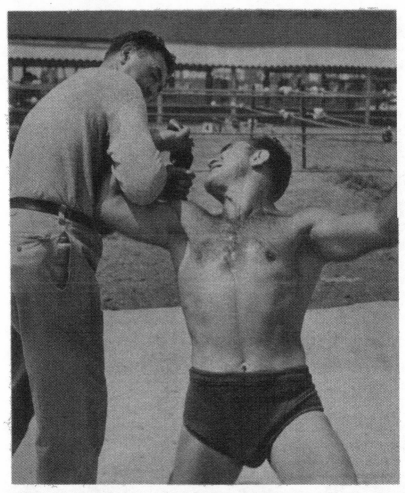

NOW, with the firm grip I have just gained, I force his gun hand back, and swing around with my right arm. With my right arm, I pin his arm against my body, and put the pressure of my chest against his arm so that I can almost break his crooked elbow across my inserted right arm. Under this pressure and pain, he cannot offer effective resistance as, with my left hand, I wrench the gun from his hand. Then I go to work on him.

Lesson 6

PETTY OFFICER FIRST CLASS

THE UNBREAKABLE STRANGLE

IF YOU aren't armed, and the enemy is not armed, and you have the luck to come up behind him, then the photos in this chapter will demonstrate what you can do to subdue or, if necessary, kill him.

The movements I outline may look difficult at first, but, like anything else, they can be mastered only by constant practice, with unending emphasis on speed. But it is a speed synchronized with good judgment and ingenuity at all times.

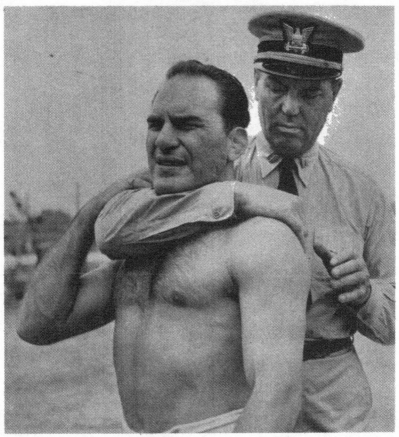

IT IS the natural impulse of most persons who aim to use a stranglehold, to grab with their fingers. Don't try to get a grip like that if you have a chance for a stranglehold with your arms. I've already shown how a finger-strangle can be broken, whether it is a front or back strangle. But the stranglehold herewith illustrated is one that nobody can break, even if you weigh only 125 pounds and the enemy scales more than 200. In this particular photo, I circle the neck of the enemy with my right arm. I press my forearm, meanwhile, against his Adam's apple. (Editor's Note: This is the cover picture.)

THEN I drop my left arm—the **upper part**—on the other man's shoulder, and lock my hold around his **neck by gripping my upper** left arm with the fingers of my right hand.

A T THIS point, I place my left hand and forearm on the back
of his head and apply pressure as I tighten the arm clamp
around his throat. You will note that I exert a vise-like grip by
pulling down hard on his left shoulder.

NOW we go into the last phase of this grip. There isn't anything the enemy can do about this, but take as much as you are inclined to deal out. And if you deal it very long, he will collapse at that point, I haul him in.

CHIEF PETTY OFFICER

DISARMING YOUR OPPONENT

"SHOOT first! Ask questions afterward."

This tough fighting motto is justly famous, and its application can be boon or bane, depending upon who has the advantage.

Never underestimate your foe. He's not very likely to ask you the time of day if you are unarmed and he isn't. It would be much more realistic to expect him to "shoot first."

That is exactly what Chief Bo'sn's Mate Bill Linder, who enacts the role of the enemy in this chapter, intends to do. He knows that dead Americans can't talk Nazis out of shooting them. So he starts to draw his gun out of his holster. If I'm the least bit slow to act, Bill will have me covered, and I will be in a bad spot. But this time I'm fast. I have to be.

THE split second I see him reach, I make a grab for his right wrist. Before he can train the gun on me, he must reach down for it, grab hold of it, pull it up and aim it. All I have to do is swoop down with my left hand and seize his wrist as he wraps his fingers around the butt of his weapon. So, if I'm tough and fast, the chances are greatly in my favor.

EVEN as I am reaching for his right wrist, I am driving my right arm into the "V" shaped opening between his wrist and shoulder. The position of his elbow as he grabs for his gun makes this possible. I knock his arm high up, so that if he has gained a hold on the gun I would jolt it from his hand.

THEN I quickly pull back my right hand and slip my left arm under his right armpit. This quick action is extremely important, as I demonstrate in the next picture.

FOR it enables me to bend his right arm back in a crushing hold at the same time that I am bending down his head. You can already see his gun-grip weakening.

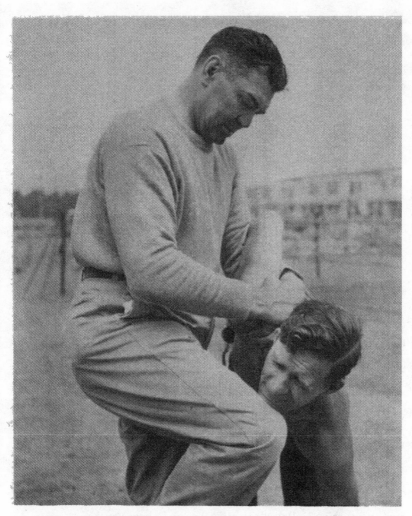

I KEEP pushing his head down until it is in range of my knee. I can afford to take no chances. I give him the knee to the face or jaw with full force. If there is any fight left in him, that will take it out. Disarming him at that point is like taking candy from a baby. But, unlike a baby, you never show the enemy mercy. Never. You must fight tough—or die!

BOATSWAIN'S MATE

BEATING THE PUNCH

I T IS agreed by the wisest of the military strategists that the best defensive is an offensive. Beating the enemy to the punch is the literal definition of such a defense.

You do not have to be a professional boxer to profit from this lesson. As a matter of fact it is intended for men who are not good with their fists, and who would probably lose if they decided to slug it out with the enemy.

Your problem is created when the enemy shoves his left hand against your chest, and cocks his right hand with the purpose of brushing you off by means of a well timed punch on the jaw. Remember that you are no pugilistic match for him. So what can you do in such a situation? Pay close attention as I show you.

(*Chief Bo'sn's Mate Cosneck again takes the part of the enemy in this lesson.*)

I'M NOT speaking as a former heavyweight champion now, but as a Coast Guardsman who has never put on a boxing glove. Yet I make it a short fight and a snappy one. I gain the initiative —which is all-important—by clamping onto the enemy's hand as he presses it against my chest.

IF THE enemy's hand isn't quite pressed against my chest, but is extended and slightly away from me, I grab for it, press it against my chest, clamp both my hands over it, and then bend forward with my body. With this movement, I put all the weight I can into the downward pressure. The enemy is in for a lot of grief, and I know better than to spare the pressure. In Commando warfare, the golden rule is, "Do unto your enemy what he would do unto you. Do it first and do it harder."

ONE of two things will happen once I've clamped the enemy's hand against my chest. If he will not lower his body toward the ground, I will break his arm or wrist. If he does the natural thing, and follows the downward pressure of that arm with his body and head, I bring his head within range of my knee and bump him. And I bump him for keeps, because I don't want any further trouble from him. This trick is usually sufficient to knock cold 99 out of 100 men. An enemy knocked cold is one enemy you don't have to worry about.

FAIR play is the last thing you should expect from the enemy. Like you, he fights tough, but much more ruthlessly. In this photo, the enemy plans to put you out of commission with a vicious kick in the groin. Don't try to block that kick with one hand. The kick may carom off and land on the target. That would leave you squirming on the ground in excruciating pain, and put you utterly at his mercy. Block with both hands, but be sure that they are crossed—as illustrated—in the form of an "X."

THE force of the kick may automatically **cause your hands to** grip the leg, as I do here. But if it **doesn't, you'll be clamping** the leg anyhow. If you fail to do that, **the block will prove only a** temporary advantage that soon **might be overcome.**

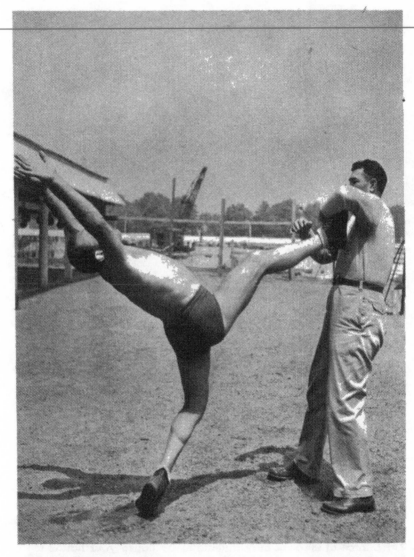

HAVING clamped the leg, jerk it upward—as savagely as you can—and flip the enemy on his back. The higher you flip him, the greater will be the injury he will suffer when he lands.

Lesson 9

MACHINIST'S MATE

SEARCHING A CAPTURED MAN

APTURING an enemy is only half a Commando's job, often less if he is not careful. Holding the enemy in custody and searching him open up new problems.

As ever, you must be tough. But toughness alone will not avail, nor will toughness be possible if you do not exert the utmost care. I will demonstrate, in this chapter, how easy it is for you to lose your prisoner if you do not act properly and at precisely the correct moment.

For example, you have made a prisoner of the enemy. You want to search him.

If you leave him standing up, with one hand holding a gun on him, and the other frisking him, he is liable to make some fast movement while you are out of quick shooting position, and turn the tables on you.

But that can't happen if you search him as do Coast Guardsmen. They take no chances.

YOU have made your capture and you have the gun on the enemy's back. The one thought uppermost in his mind—as it would be in yours if the positions were reversed—is escape. Never forget that, and guide yourself accordingly. Always expect a false move, and be careful not to make one. Order your captive to face and lean against a wall, a post or a tree (in this case represented by the ropes of a boxing ring).

MAKE him cross his hands, and command him to step back several paces while he is leaning against whatever object (among those listed under the previous photo) happens to be handy. Then have him cross his feet, and force him to keep his body stretched and rigid. Don t let him relax or sag at the knees. Thus his potential striking power is reduced to a minimum, as his body is now extended in an unnatural position.

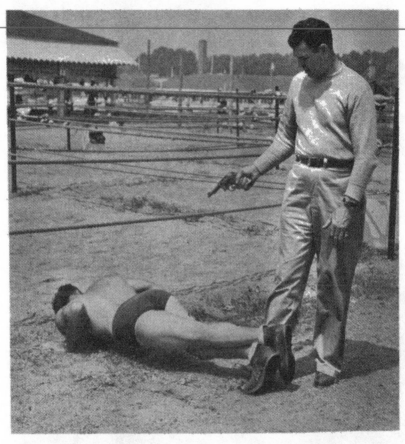

THAT is not to say that he may not try some funny business. The point is that as long as you have him in that position, he cannot attempt any trickery without first giving you a warning by uncrossing his hands, or uncrossing his feet. That's the time for you to get tough. The very fraction of a second that you see him trying anything like that, kick at his shin bones with all your might. This will send his legs flying upward, cause him to lose his leaning support, and make him fall down on his face. After he picks up his teeth and spits the dirt out of his mouth, he won't be further disposed to challenge your advantage or to attempt escape.

Lesson 10

HAMMERING YOUR WAY OUT OF A STRANGLEHOLD

QUARTERMASTER

I HAVE said before, and I now repeat, that it is absolutely foolhardy to underestimate the enemy. He is not only a killer, but a cunning and ruthless killer. You must be prepared to cope with him under any circumstances, and the only way you can prepare effectively to do that is to anticipate any conceivable initiative he might take against you.

In a previous chapter, I demonstrated how to break a front hold on your throat by thrusting your arms up between those of the enemy who is choking you. But suppose the enemy had his arms so close together that you couldn't force your arms between the small opening?

ASSUME that he grabs you by the neck, as Bernard Cosneck does to me in this photo. Obviously he means business, and if I do not act quickly I will be a dead pigeon, because bringing them back alive is not part of the Axis creed. While I wince with pain, I do not shut my eyes. I notice that the space between the inside of his arms is very narrow.

THIS presents a difficult task, but not an impossible one. I suddenly shoot up high with my right arm, on the outside of his
left. I have complete freedom of motion, since, in order to impede
the thrust of my right arm, the enemy would have to relax his grip
around my neck. He has only one chance.

INSTEAD, of course, he tightens his stranglehold. My move had better be good, or it's curtains. Remember, all this happens much more quickly than the time it takes to explain it. It all occurs in the space of a few short seconds. Having brought up my right arm in the manner described on the previous page, I then bring it down with a hammer stroke on the enemy's right arm. I don't try to crash both his arms at the same time. It's harder to break down two than one. I hammer on his right arm with my right. Sometimes one solid smash might do the trick. At any rate, I continue twisting my body to the right, thus enclosing the enemy's both arms in my right arm. Then I reach up with my left hand and break one of his little fingers. This may sound cruel, but bear in mind that a Nazi with a broken finger isn't going to sneak up on any American and choke him to death.

Lesson 11

SIGNALMAN

BREAKING A BACK CHOKE

NEVER be surprised if the enemy comes up at you from behind. Experience has taught us that that is the favorite method of Axis attack, whether by a battalion of men or by a lone soldier. A sporting chance represents a philosophy which the dictator nations absolutely do not understand.

If an unarmed enemy sneaks up on you from the rear, he is likely to strike you where it will do the most harm in the least time. Choking an unsuspecting American from the back would be any Nazi's pleasure.

You must fight tough to deny the enemy this indulgence at the expense of your skin.

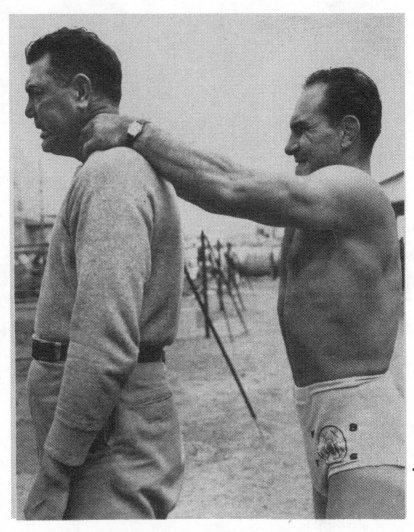

I HAVE been caught unawares by the enemy. Attacking from behind, he has seized a powerful grip on my throat. He cleverly keeps his distance so that I can't reach back with my arms. Nor is he near enough for a backward kick in the groin or shins to take effect. My predicament demands quick thinking.

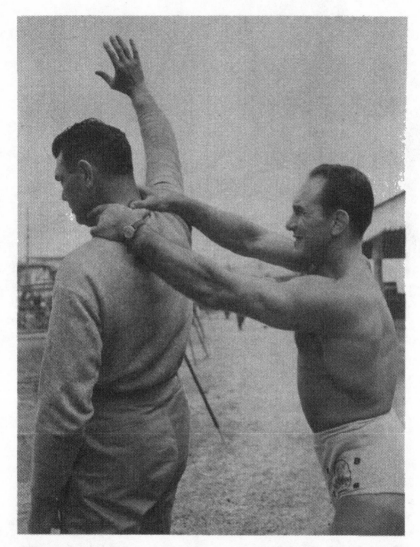

THERE is only one way out. In such a situation, I raise my right arm high. If he thinks I am heiling Hitler, he is in for a sorry awakening. He is, as a matter of fact, in for a sorry awakening no matter what he thinks.

AS I RAISE my right arm, I pivot sharply toward the flabber-gasted enemy, and bring my arm sweeping down on top of his. It is not for nothing that he wears that disturbed look on his face. He'll soon think a truncheon hit him.

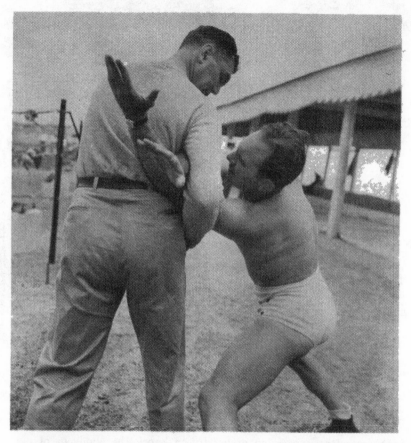

WHEN the latter motion is completed, I have reversed the situation and the enemy is now in my power, as you can see. My right hand is grasping my left wrist, giving me a complete lock on my opponent. By exerting maximum pressure, I can break one or both of the man's arms, or flip him over on his back. If I prefer, I can shift my leg position, then trip and throw him to the ground. This is by way of showing that once you have shaken off the strangle and gained the drop on the enemy, you can do with him as you please. He is in a completely helpless situation. I intend to keep him that way.

ELECTRICIAN'S MATE

STRANGLEHOLD ALTERNATIVE

ANYTHING is cricket in war. You must take your opportunities where you find them. For any variety of reasons, it might be necessary and wise to attack the enemy from the rear. More than likely he'll be retreating. But whatever his purpose, even though his back is to you, he means no good. While his back may be turned toward you, his bayonet or gun may be poking in the belly of a fellow American. You can understand that it is not only cricket, but good fighting and an expression of loyalty to knock the wind out of his sails. Assuming that you have the will—and without the will, I might point out, your life isn't worth two cents—I will teach you the way.

S HOULD you be fortunate enough to slip up behind the enemy, as I do in this picture, you can apply the stranglehold which I demonstrated previously. But should it be difficult for you to grab his throat, secure him firmly around the waist with your left arm. My follow-up must come promptly.

ACTING quickly—for speed still means the difference between life and death in Commando warfare—I then reach down with my right hand and grab his ankle. And I grab it hard, because I cannot afford a slip-up, lest I lose my advantage.

WITH a firm grip on his ankle, I am now able to lift his leg. As I do so, I prop my left leg against his thigh and maintain a firm hold around his waist with my left hand. This combination of throttling holds paralyzes the enemy for the moment—a moment long enough to permit me eventually to dispose of him.

WHILE I have this hold on his right leg, I quickly thrust my left leg between his legs. I curve my left leg around his left leg, hold his right leg back to put him in a spinning position, and proceed to trip him, face first, to the earth.

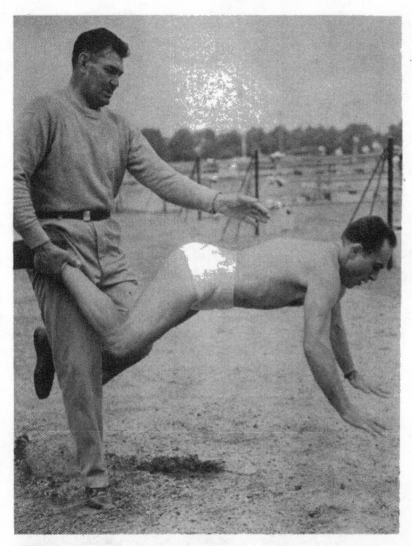

THIS is just what the doctor ordered, as it sends the bewildered enemy sprawling to the ground on all fours. Just in case he did not have enough momentum for his fall, I give him an added push with my left hand to guarantee results.

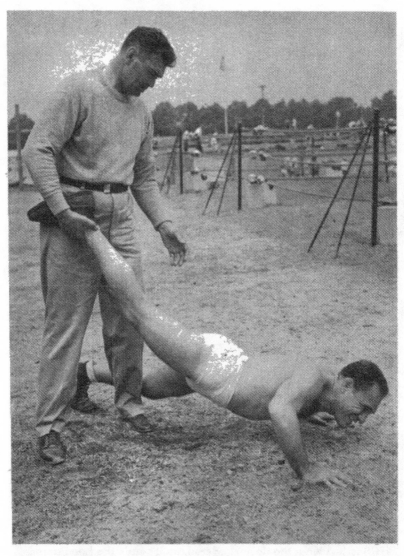

YOU will notice that all the while he is hurtling to the ground, I never release my hold on the enemy's right ankle. I cling to this important advantage even as he hits the earth.

NOW you can see the reason for holding onto his right ankle. I fall upon the enemy and drive the knee of my left leg against the inside knee of his right leg. I switch my grip from his ankle to his foot and press it forward. Then I clamp his foot with my right knee. By exerting sufficient pressure on the imprisoned foot, I leave my hands free for other activity.

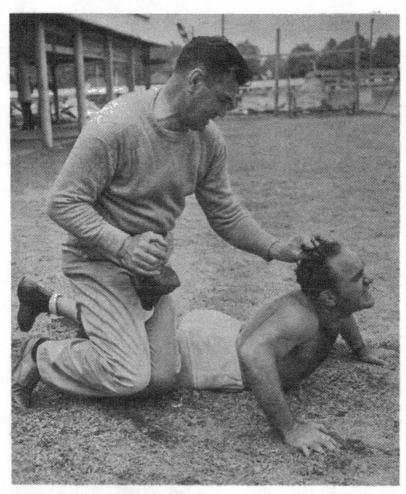

THIS is a sample of the "other activity." While waiting for
someone to come along and haul him away, you can amuse
yourself thus by tearing at the hair of the enemy. If he is bald-
headed, you will have to devise some other form of entertainment.
Amusing? Perhaps, but the jokes are grim and few and far
between in Commando warfare. And it is just as easy to be the
butt of one as the perpetrator.

C

COOK

THE BELT TRICK

B Y NOW it should be apparent that fighting tough is not only a necessity but an art. There is no end to the number of tricks and short cuts a Commando employs in order to deal with the enemy.

Every part of the enemy's person can be converted to your advantage if you are versed well enough in fighting tough to recognize the right thing to do at the right moment.

One of the most ingenious, and one well worth keeping in mind, is the belt trick. You may run up against a condition in which the enemy is not wearing a coat, in which case you cannot resort to the lapel-jerking trick described earlier. That's where the belt trick comes in. For in all likelihood he will be wearing a belt of some kind—a belt on his trousers, or a belt on his bathing suit.

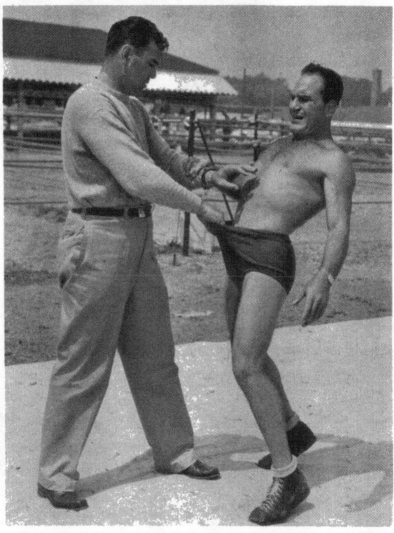

WHEN you go to work on the belt trick you must move alertly. Before the enemy has a chance to realize what you're up to, grab his belt or a handful of clothes at the waist and jerk it toward you while keeping him at bay.

COORDINATION of movement is very essential to fighting tough. In the belt trick, for instance, at the same moment that you seize the enemy's belt, you drive your left forearm against his throat. This wards off all reprisals.

YOU follow this up by stepping behind him with your left foot and bending him backward over your left knee. You are now in command of the situation. You may use your own judgment as to the next procedure.

IF THE enemy goes after you with a knife, he's not bluffing. He means to cut you deep and painfully—fatally if possible. He will use the knife in one of three ways—the downward stroke illustrated on this page, the upward stroke demonstrated on the next page; or, if he is a cunning knife wielder, he will use the inside stroke, with the knife held along his chest. I will discuss how to deal with the latter stroke in the next chapter. Meanwhile, look at the photo on this page again, and assume that the enemy is trying to slash down at you with his knife. Immediately block it by raising your left forearm against his right forearm, poising your right hand for supplemental action.

A S YOU ram his right forearm with your left forearm, you exert every ounce of additional pressure you can and force his arm down until it is in this position, with the knife pointed toward you, but not as likely to make contact.

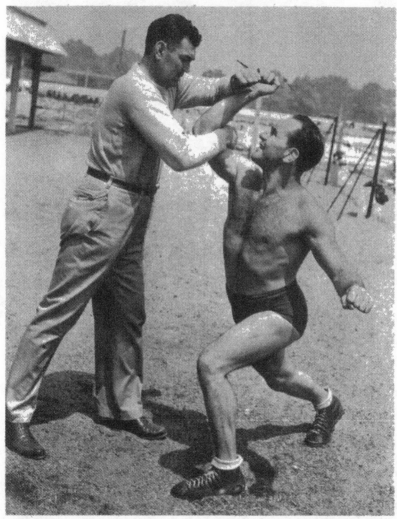

YOU quickly swing your right forearm around and lodge it inside the enemy's elbow. At the same time, your left forearm is still pressed against your adversary's right forearm, and you force his arm back to a point approximating his original striking position. Then you're in the homestretch.

THAT accomplished, you press back and down on the
enemy's right forearm with your left forearm until you have
locked his arm in a vise. After that, rough him up without the
slightest compunction, because, at worst, you'll be giving him
only a little of what he had in store for you. A kick in the groin
at this juncture will definitely eliminate his nuisance value. I
want to point out that this exercise, like all the others, is one
in which speed is vital for success. The trick must be practised
regularly to get the knack of coordination. Once it is well
learned, the whole action becomes automatic.

RADIOMAN

FOOLING THE SMART KNIFE MAN

I KNOW of no worse way of meeting disaster than at the point of a knife. And just as certainly, I know that the enemy thinks nothing of slashing you to ribbons if you give him the opportunity.

I teach Coast Guardsmen how to protect themselves in any eventuality involving the use of a knife by the enemy. In the previous chapter, I dealt with an assailant who attacks with either the downward or upward stroke.

In this chapter, posed by two of my assistants, I demonstrate how to ward off the most dangerous knife attack of all—the assault in which the knife is held inside, on a level with the user's chest.

Chief Bo'sn's Mate Bernard Cosneck, in the black tights, takes the defensive against Chief Bo'sn's Mate Mario Ghiselli, who fought in the ring under the name of Matty Mario before he joined the Coast Guard and became a member of my staff.

WHEN a knife is held in this position—inside on a level with the chest—it is not possible to charge in on the enemy if you are unarmed yourself without the danger that he will slash you from left to right, or up or down.

BUT Chief Bo'sn's Mate Cosneck has been schooled to meet the situation. If the enemy wants to play rough, he found the right man. Cosneck, realizing that it is his skin or the enemy's, has a marked preference for his own. He knows exactly what he is about as he approaches the knife man from the side, feet first, and dives that way at the enemy's left leg.

THAT timely maneuver does it. The enemy falls flat on his face, and counts himself lucky that he was not stabbed by his own knife. As the enemy lights on terra firma, Cosneck plants his own left leg in front of the enemy's left ankle. At the same time, Cosneck reaches up with his right leg and vigorously drives it back of the enemy's left knee, twisting his own body around to the left.

COSNECK continues the twisting motion until he is sitting upright, and the flabbergasted enemy's left leg is wrapped in an unbreakable toe hold. This photo, baring Cosneck's tanned back to the camera, emphasizes the enemy's agony and helplessness. We prescribe this as the preferred position for the enemy at all times—at your mercy.

BUT Cosneck has been trained *not* to leave well enough alone. When dealing with a ruthless, knife wielding foe, it is the better part of discretion—and valor—to improve well enough to maximum punishment for the enemy. Accordingly, Cosneck turns on the juice and twists his captor's leg until it begins to resemble a pretzel. Groaning and writhing, the enemy is on the verge of relaxing his grip on the knife, for it has turned out to be about as useless as his left leg—which is definitely doing him no good.

Lesson 15

YEOMAN

INSTEP SMASH

THE enemy is indefatigable and you can afford to be no less. Failing to subdue you one way, he will try another and another and another. Eventually, this clash of individuals will come to a head. And there are not any no-decision bouts in war. The verdict comes—most often quite quickly—very decisively. There are no draws or exhibitions of feint-and-flee skill when the fighting Commandos are abroad. Anything goes, and most everything happens. In the final analysis, it is only speed which gives you the advantage. That is why I drill Coast Guardsmen so incessantly on the necessity for instant action. It will be these precious seconds on every fighting front of the world that will ultimately bring the Axis to its knees.

I pose in three of the five pictures in this chapter to show you how to dispose of the enemy when he gets the jump on you from behind. Then Chief Bo'sn's Mates Matty Mario and Andy Filosa take over the lens to illustrate a hard and effective maneuver which we call, "Knee to Face."

THE enemy has jumped me from behind, caught me flat footed.
I must think and act quickly. He may try a stranglehold. He
may try to trip me. He may try anything. Instinctively, I snap my
body forward. Because he has a hold on me, his body moves with
mine, and that pulls one of his insteps into position.

SO I give him the heel of my shoe with all possible force, right on the instep. He cries out in surprised pain, and tries to wrench his foot free, but he doesn't get it loose until I wish.

WHILE he is recoiling from the crushing blow on his instep, I bring my left knee as high as possible, then drive backward with my foot and aim, with all my strength, at his groin. If the smash to the instep hasn't tamed him, the kick in the groin will certainly spread him out like a door mat and make him wish he had stayed home selling wiener schnitzel. After a foot massage like this, the enemy is no good to himself or his country.

I F NEITHER you nor your enemy is armed, it is to your utmost
advantage to get the jump on him. Chief Bo'sn's Mates Matty
Mario (in the white trousers) and Andy Filosa (the enemy in black
tights) demonstrate a very effective method.

Matty doesn't give the enemy time to consider a form of attack.
He suddenly reaches out, cups his right hand back of Andy's
neck, and snaps it down while he puts thumb pressure just below
Andy's diaphragm to take the breath out of him.

THEN, as he is driving Andy's face downward, Matty hoists his right knee. This can break the enemy's skull, fracture his nose, spill his teeth, rip his lips and blind him. In short if he survives, he might safely be returned to the Fatherland where his battered recollection of a face could be used to induce recalcitrant children to heil the Fuehrer.

STOREKEEPER

TURNING
THE TABLES WITH A BAYONET

IT IS a very simple thing for an unarmed man to stop a bayonet with his stomach. It is not so easy to stand up to an enemy rushing at you with a bayonet in his hand, and to disarm this man charging ahead with steely death.

Speed, as you may well imagine, is of paramount importance. One second's delay in springing to action may easily cost your life. And the fields of battle are already littered with the bodies of many who lost their lives at the price of slow reflexes.

In these illustrations, Matty Mario takes the part of the enemy with a bayonet, while Andy Filosa is on the defensive.

Matty charges at Andy with the bayonet. What happens to Andy, who is unarmed, depends entirely upon Andy's speed of hands and feet. If he can move with the swiftness that is taught at the U. S. Coast Guard Station at Manhattan Beach, he has a good chance of saving himself and conquering the enemy, then ramming him with his own bayonet.

A S THE thrust is made, Andy sidesteps with great speed,
reaches out his left hand, grabs the barrel of the gun, and
points its bayoneted end away from him. So far so good, but Andy
is far from safe yet. He cannot stop here.

IMMEDIATELY Andy lunges at the enemy, grabbing more firmly at the weapon. He gets alongside him and faces the same way. Then he jams his right leg in back of the enemy's left leg. By pulling back on the gun on which he now has a vise-like grip, it is a simple matter to trip the bayonet-toting enemy.

A S THE enemy flies through the air, he will relax completely
or loosen his grip on the bayonet. Andy quickly takes pos-
session of the weapon as the enemy lands on the ground. These
are the enemy's last moments. You do not make believe with
bayonets. It is kill or be killed. Now the would-be killer is des-
tined to lose his life as he intended to take another's. Andy
plunges down into the enemy's face with the head or handle of
the gun. If this does not persuade the enemy that he is waging a
lost battle, and nothing is to be gained from bringing him back
alive, Andy reverses the gun and stabs the enemy with the
bayoneted end. Dead enemies do not trouble you again.

Coast Guardsmen are taught not to try to use the bayonet end first. They would lose time in doing that. They have the handle of the gun almost in the face of the enemy as he falls. The immediate jab with the hard and heavy butt of the gun may subdue the man who, otherwise, might roll away, jump up and escape before the gun could be reversed and the bayonet end could be used.

PHARMACIST'S MATE

BREAKING A STAND-OFF

THE boys at the United States Coast Guard station at Manhattan Beach are intensively drilled in how to handle an enemy with or without a weapon. They take turns at being the enemy, and, after a while, it is tough for one to subdue the other because each knows the standard tricks.

That is where individual judgment and ingenuity come into play, where speed tells and alertness prevails. For ultimately, in this as in all struggles, every man winds up on his own.

What Coast Guardsmen do under these circumstances is, I think, very interesting and instructive. Not only are they called upon to originate tricks of their own to meet the exigencies of the moment, but they often resort to old-time tricks.

One of these ancient maneuvers is revived in this chapter illustrated by Andy Filosa and Matty Mario.

BEING equally **wise in the ways of** Commando **tactics, neither** is able to seize an early **advantage over** the other. **Neither** will venture close enough to the other to leave himself vulnerable to a kick in the groin or the knee. So each grabs the other's hands and holds each other off. But obviously they cannot go on waltzing like this forever.

S OMETHING like this was bound to happen sooner or later. Both men were watching catlike for an opportunity to spring at the other. Andy strikes first as he suddenly grabs Matty's right wrist with both of his own, whirls in toward Matty, faces the same way as Matty, and then pulls Matty forward and onto his back. This is an old wrestling stunt, and it's good to know when you reach a stalemate with a killer.

O OOPS! There goes Matty. Andy hurls the enemy through
the air with the greatest of ease, and with no concern over
what happens when Matty hits the ground. Remember, in actual
combat there is no mat to cushion the descent of the enemy—nor
your own! Either you fall hard or you hit hard.

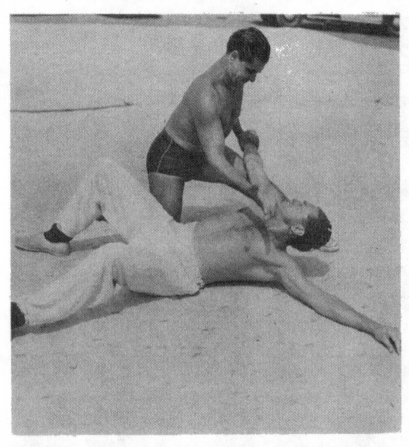

S TILL retaining his hold on the enemy's arm, Andy goes to his knees on the floor and places Matty's right arm over his left knee and bends it down. If Matty tries to struggle away from that, any slight added pressure by Andy will break the arm. In coping with the actual enemy, be assured that this "slight added pressure" will prove very helpful. When you fight tough, you think no more of fracturing the enemy's arm than punching him on the nose. You fracture their arms in ten places if necessary. The Axis invented the medicine. Let them swallow it. It will kill or cure them, mark my words.

COMMISSARY STEWARD

DOUBLE WRIST-LOCK

WITH this chapter, we conclude the carefully selected and pains-takingly analyzed lessons in "How to Fight Tough."

In the words of President Roosevelt, "This is the toughest war of all time." It will, therefore, be won by the toughest fighters of all time. And when the final score is chalked up, the best fighters will prove the toughest.

For being tough in Commando warfare is not a simple thing. It does not mean merely the application of stupid brute force, as the Nazis and Japs suppose. It does not mean sheer sadism. It does not mean bombing civilian populations. It does not mean raping women. It does not mean maiming children. It does not mean bullying of the weak by the strong.

To an American, fighting the most crucial battle of freedom in the world's history, being tough means protecting the American heritage of dignity and freedom—freedom of thought, of speech, of action, of press, of education, of sports and of religion—for all men, a freedom that protects our right to indulge or refrain without imposing, by physical force or any kind of coercion, our views or habits upon others.

LESSON 18 *continued*

That is something worth fighting tough for. That is why Americans will emerge the toughest fighters of all. When a Coast Guardsman strangles a Nazi, he will know that he is driving a nail in the coffin of tyranny. He will not kill for the lust of killing, as does his enemy. When a Coast Guardsman plunges a bayonet into a Jap's belly, it will not be for joy of seeing blood run—an unbearable Nipponese pastime—but to stop sooner the flow of blood from the veins of free and innocent men the world over who have been crushed in a heroic effort to stay the onward march of the Axis steamroller.

It will be the individual American soldier who finally puts that steamroller out of operation. He will not do it by trying to push it back in its path. That can't be done. He will do it, so to speak, by climbing up in the driver's seat and flinging the pilot to his death.

If soldiers in every branch of the service—including those now in uniform and those about to don them—will study and practice this course, I am confident that this book will, in years to come, be able to make the proud boast that it was responsible for a lion's share of dead Japs and Nazis and Fascists.

Fantastic and melodramatic as it may seem, I would like to see the day when Hitler and Hirohito and Mussolini meet their respective dooms at the trained hands of lone Americans, and that when their assassins show themselves, there will be found in their hip pockets a copy of this book.

For I firmly believe that if we fight tough today, we will be able to live peacefully tomorrow. Not otherwise.

THE double wrist-lock is one of the most popular in wrestling. I teach it with variations. In this photo, I am going through the first process of a wrist-lock on Bernard Cosneck.

Y OU will find this hold very useful in dealing with obstreperous
Nazis and Japs. In the second process, in the application
of the double wrist-lock, I keep a firm grip on the enemy's right
hand with my right hand, and strengthen this hold by bringing to
bear at the same point of contact my left hand, which snakes
under his shoulder pit to his wrist.

YOUR enemy will whimper like a spanked baby when you complete the operation of the double wrist-lock, as illustrated in this photo. I have both his hands locked up now, and what I am doing to the little finger of his right hand for good measure is nothing for faint-hearted persons to contemplate.

BUT I'm still not through with the enemy. While retaining a grip on the wrist, I slide my right hand off his wrist, and down his right hand. Then, if his fingers are not opened, I force him to open them. He'll either open them or loose them.

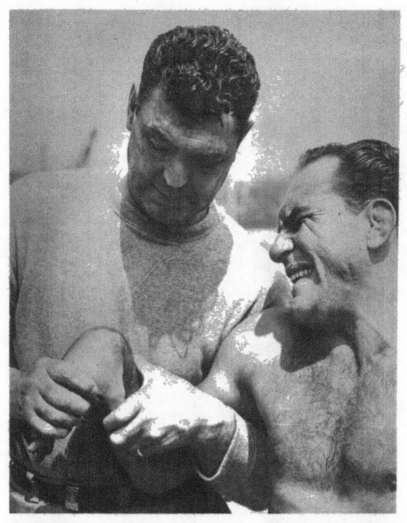

THERE is a very good reason why I have not gripped his thumb, but left it standing alone. If you will study this photo carefully, you will notice that while I am pulling four fingers one way, I am pulling the thumb the other way. If I continue to increase the pressure, one or all of his fingers are bound to break.

IF I elect to do so, I can split the thumb with one hand and break the little finger with the other, by bending them in different directions. Either method is guaranteed to incapacitate the enemy—no matter how tough he is—and, at the same time render him helpless. If he is foolish enough to try to struggle, I simply apply more pressure, and I begin to hear the cracking of Nazi bones. Hard? Ruthless? You think so? Remember—you've got to fight tough to survive this war. We're up against the toughest, most savage array of nations in history. If we're not tougher than they, we'll be licked. *We'll be tougher.*

Epilogue

I WOULD like to leave a few final words with all young American men, in the service or about to join, who read and keep this book.

This book is not written for your entertainment. It was produced for your guidance. At home and abroad, war is serious business and represents a constant threat to life and limb. You never know when you may be called upon to use the holds explained in "How to Fight Tough."

This is a tough book because it is a guide for tough men. You might just as well not read it at all as read it once and forget about it. Read it again and again. And practice the lessons again and again until you do them as automatically as you drive an automobile.

Train yourself to think quickly and to act more quickly.

Then you will know "How to Fight Tough."

The End

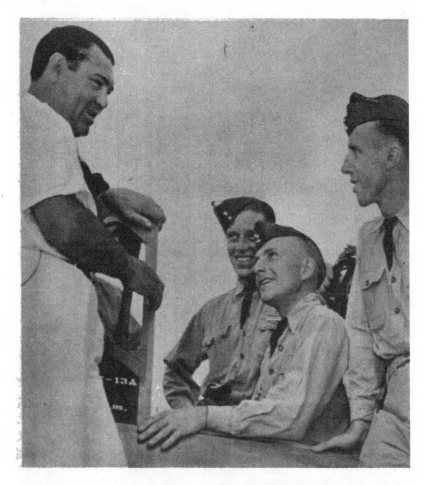

EVEN before he was commissioned a Lieutenant in the United States Coast Guard, the former heavyweight champion of the world displayed a keen, active interest in the condition of our armed forces. Dempsey, who was awake to the nation's peril long before Pearl Harbor, is seen swapping stories with British aviation cadets at Gunter Field, Alabama, on October 15, 1941. At that time Dempsey warned these British allies, "You've got to fight tough to win this war."

E AGER and admiring faces of Coast Guard recruits light up
as the former Manassa Mauler swings into his new job—
teaching American warriors how to fight tough. As Dempsey
gives a pep talk to his men, he is surrounded by a host of ring
luminaries, including heavyweight Nathan Mann in the long-
trouser sweat outfit; Marty Servo, next to Mann, and Lou Ambers,
beside Dempsey. The boxers were instructors for a day.

STILL affectionately known as "The Champ," Lieutenant Dempsey approaches his new job with the same sincerity and singlemindedness of purpose that once won for him the cherished heavyweight crown. He flashes footwork reminiscent of the olden days as an unarmed "foe" tries unsuccessfully to grab his rifle. He grabs trouble instead.

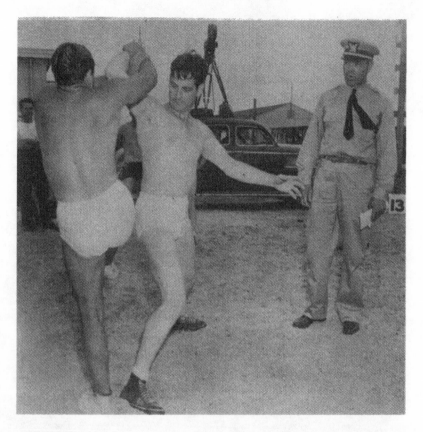

THE author of "How to Fight Tough" looks on with interest as a pair of Coast Guardsmen pupils tangle in a training session. "Remember," cautions Dempsey, "he's the enemy. Break off his arm and hit him over the head with it!"